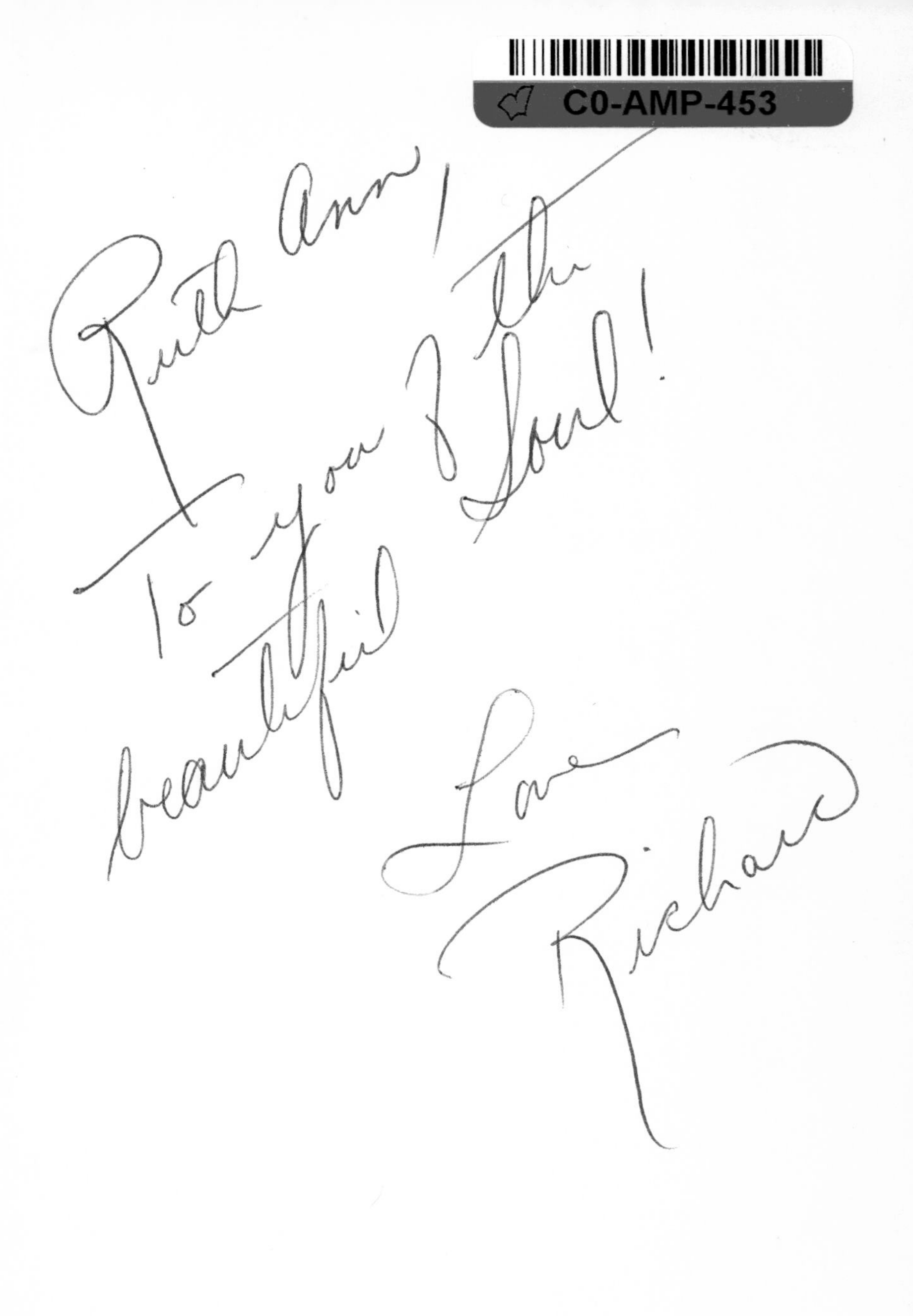
C0-AMP-453
Ruth Ann,
To you & the
beautiful Soul!
Love
Richard

My Soul Remembers

My Soul Remembers

by

Richard Dale Billings

A
Parker
Book

Arnold Press, Inc. **Tulsa, Oklahoma**

My Soul Remembers

To
a love I shared
and will long remember

My Soul Remembers

Time
Yesterday
Tomorrow
Love
Prayer
Life
Death
Freedom
Truth
Success
Christ
Fear
Karma
Humility
Children
Evening
The Sun
The Calendar
The Christ Pattern
The Nun's Prayer
The Seasons
America

A GIFT

by Richard Dale Billings

God gave you me for a little while
Like a gentle breeze,
Like a friendly smile.
God in all His goodness knows
The path we should follow,
And our way He shows.
Our separate paths He made to cross;
Time is eternity.
Nothing is lost.

I'll long remember, I won't forget.
A love I shared,
A love I let.
Out of the past it came to me;
A love that I loved
Yet would be free.
Warmly, I hold it in my heart
A memory in consciousness
We are not apart.

INTRODUCING
A PATH TO UNDERSTANDING

The word understanding is often misunderstood. To understand is to stand under that which you believe and support with your thoughts and energy. You lend this support until that which you believe is able to stand alone. We need to get under the blanket of thought and uncover our thinking so we can support it unhampered.

A path is a route we follow which carries us along the shortest distance to our desired destination. Let us travel this path to understanding together and gather what insight we find along the journey.

The eternal path is the path we walk together in thought and prayer. It is in this realm we enjoy oneness, and there can be no separation.

Soul is the accumulated thoughts and feelings of our many lifetimes of sharing. Soul is the tape recorder of the universe that receives, records, transmits, and plays back the knowledge of all previous incarnations.

Through the action of mind, the body becomes a reactor to the impulses of thought vibrations. Upon the tape of memory is told the endless story of man's walk through eternity.

This book contains material that might appear controversial to the consciously unaware or those reluctant to let go of the bind of tradition. It may have a revolutionary approach to life, but life is revolutionary. Man must come into recognition that the old ways must be overthrown so freedom can reign. Freedom comes through growth and understanding. Many lifetimes are required for men to learn lessons and adjust mentally, physically, and spiritually.

Reincarnation is God's method of allowing man to work out his salvation. Man moves through many bodies, male and female, wears many colors, and is labeled with nationalities. In the final analysis he will know there is only ONE!

We are on this path to build consciousness. Now is the time for a revival in consciousness so the warring can be eliminated in the body and revival expanded into our world. The armies of fear, disease, sin, death, and poverty march like mighty warriors until a consciousness of love comes forth to claim her victory. The time has come for the triumphal entry of love into the city of peace.

I will travel as your guide through the pages of this book. I go as the first person, introducing you to personalities the soul has remembered. Together we travel, yet free to make our own evaluation. At the close of the journey we will discover what we are today is a composite of many lives. This is the law of expansion at work; each lifetime brings greater depth to the soul nature.

If there are questions, this is good. A mind in search will find answers. As the covers are closed you may know a new you. Disturbing habits that have plagued you may find clarification. The Infinite reveals herself to each of us in her own unique way. Understand this is my revelation, yours will be distinctive to your own soul development. Walk the path of life with me in prayer and understanding that we might be one with each other and one with our God in eternal love. Rest in the realization that time is telling her story, and you are a part of it. Move with life; stop resisting, for the currents of love are moving through the universe to heal, bless, restore, and prosper all mankind. May God grant you, each one, the good desires of your heart. I am your friend; you are my brother.

RDB

Man is reminiscent of his yesterdays, but what is yesterday?

Yesterday is only a flash in the fleeting movement of time.

Time is, just as God is, eternal and not subject to definition.

Man has given time a label as he has many things in his world.

The events in this eternal motion leave an indelible imprint upon the ethers of the universe.

All action is recorded in order to thrust man into what he refers to as the future.

However, man is not always able to move into the future for he retains the past and is unable to consciously release it.

* * *

My soul remembers, and the search begins for answers.

Spirit haunts the past to explain the present in her quest for understanding.

Paul felt this when he wrote to the Romans, "Let every soul be subject unto the higher powers. For there is no power but of God: the powers that be are ordained of God." (Romans 13:1)

The soul must seek this lofty realm in order to receive Divine Inspiration and Illumination. Universal law must be understood, and man must be obedient to its action for it is action unto itself.

In Romans 13:10, Paul informs us, "Love worketh no ill to his neighbour: therefore love is the fulfilling of the law."

Love sits on the seat of justice and tries her case until the action is adjusted to the reaction of love in transforming all that is unlike God into the image and likeness of God as Infinite Love.

I ask, "How many yesterdays have I lived in order to realize today?"

I hear about tomorrow; but what is tomorrow?

I tell you, tomorrow is only an extension of what man calls today.

Today is the only time I seem to know; I am not quite acquainted with tomorrow.

Yesterday has left me with only a memory.

Tomorrow is beckoning, but today—yes, today, is my friend.

* * *

Today, I stand before my world, unsure, questioning, for life has conditioned me regarding man's beliefs and concepts.

I stand before that which is greater than self yet an integral part of me.

In my longing to know, I stand before the eternal, naked, free from flesh and free from possessions.

These are vital moments in consciousness when man has communion with the Infinite.

My soul is a constant reminder that a world calls, duty demands, and life is insistent.

There are times when I stand as a part of the whole, but only for minutes, sometimes only for seconds.

The greater portion of life spent in a body is a form of isolation and separateness that invites fear and doubt to the unknowing.

In these dark moments, I am reminded of the words of the Psalmist as he said, "Trust in the Lord, and do good; so shalt thou dwell in the land, and verily thou shalt be fed." (Psalms 37:3)

In my searching, I have scanned the heavens; I have found solace under her subtle blanket that wraps a majesty about the universe and sparkles with extravagance.

I have arrived at this conclusion: life is not controlled by the stars, but by that which put the stars in their orbit.

The solar system is part of His plan just as we, too, are included in the great scheme of things.

I am intrigued with the order and regularity

of our solar system and wonder how long it will take us to comprehend this order.

We say the sun rises, but traveling with the sun we would prove this a false concept.

As people, when we accept confinement to a body, our world is limited.

We are unable to go beyond this outline and touch the eternal.

I remember a time as I stood, in the glory of a sunset, and watched her golden threads cast a path across a quiet ocean to me; she was regal as she disappeared beyond the horizon; her movement studied, disciplined and almost haughty.

The rays mingled with the cells of my being, and I took her into myself for warmth and healing.

There was an exchange of energy and an inner excitement as I watched the flaming display, which unequaled any sight I had ever seen.

The sun knows so well and senses with her pentrating illumination the great emptiness in me as she gently sinks into another part of our universe.

My desire was to blend with the magnificent display; I was reluctant to let her go.

In a last goodbye, I heard her whisper, "I'll see you, in what you call, tomorrow."

* * *

Now, it is evening.

Evening is gentle, quiet, and unmistakably, a time for soul remembrance.

I open my arms to you, evening, and accept your cloak of softness as comfort.

Moonlight, starlight, how awesome is your beauty, yet so unpretentious.

I look at you and know this is God.

God in all His splendor—a panorama bigger than self and too vast for comprehension.

* * *

Searching the sky, I am reminded of Infinite energy and the eternal action of mind, as it evolves a world and all that it contains, in the manifest form.

God, All-Knowing Mind, when rightly understood, contains inexhaustible supply.

Man must learn how to extract his good from the one and only source and man must be resourceful in the shaping and molding of Divine Substance.

Our world and all it composes began in mind action just as mind action builds our bodies, maintains and sustains them.

We are mind, and the body becomes a temporary structure which we inhabit for the purpose of growing and learning through experience.

Body after body, we grow into oneness with that which we are; for the lost image is in the process of being restored.

You may ask; how do you know?

My only knowing is through the information revealed to me by the soul.

The soul in her accumulation of information is now releasing what she holds as instruction.

Now, I stand on the threshold of eternity, waiting to express God through manifestation.

* * *

Yes, eons ago it all began.

You and I have traveled through the pages of time.

From cover to cover, time has recorded events in the great books and left us the message of the Bible.

Through Bible stories, man relates himself to God as he searches for the deep meanings.

Finally, man is removing the symbol, rending the veil in order to reveal the hidden truth.

God's thoughts and words receive animation as life enters the nostrils.

This action turns man into a mobile Temple equipped to do a tremendous missionary project.

There is a plan and purpose for all creation, and each of us fits into the seeming puzzle with precise accuracy.

Life is growth, and growth is an unfolding process that brings with it discovery as well as recovery.

Acknowledge yourselves as spiritual pilgrims

engaged in the exploration of the invisible and unknown. Be awakened by the truth that one is the same as the other.

We are flexing our spiritual muscles and moving from adolescence into adult understanding.

Yes, my soul remembers, and the search continues.

Man creeps and crawls through mountains of books; he walks and staggers through volumes of written material only to be trapped by another man's thinking and unable to think for himself.

Man follows after man as he talks, lectures, and teaches.

Man builds idols and loses sight of an ideal.

It seems inevitable, but time will stop this masquerade.

Eventually, man will recognize man for what he is, not what he appears to be.

Man will be in a position to face self, realistically and honestly, without reservation.

In this total experience with self, God is revealed.

* * *

Time is not gentle in the shaping and molding of her pupils.

How well I remember and still feel her finger of discipline as she moves to correct and adjust.

Time takes us through the hills, into the valleys, across the streams, plays with us in the sunshine, and shelters us from the storm.

Over highways, byways, even many detours, Time moves with us through many lifetimes, wearing the mantle of personality, immersed in self and lost to oneness.

* * *

I ask in deep concern and with a passion to know.

How long, Lord? Why, Lord? When Lord? and again, How long, Lord?

I make my requests known.

I pray for understanding and seek to find.

I ask, being an expression of yourself, do you not feel the pain?

Do you not feel it as I feel it?

Is not my loneliness yours?

Do not my tears flow on your face as yours on mine?

Is not my aching heart your own, seeking to express love and be loved?

Tell me, life, is this not true?

I ask you. Give me answers.

Man must learn all problems have right answers.

I realize the answer is not in the problem but in the equalizer that brings a solution.

Standing on the edge of time, I announce my hunger for knowledge and guidance.

Crying and hungry, I stand, waiting to be fed.

I see before me a sleeping, slumbering world, hypnotized by its own detachment; too selfish to become involved; immune to the needs of others.

The world forgets our need is but her own need to make a contribution.

People talk much and present a number of philosophies yet they will not make a commitment regarding what they believe.

Man surveys the many fields of endeavor but never enters the field to reap the harvest.

Living on the fringe of life, man is afraid to be a creative witness to it.

In a human way, we have been lured into avoiding responsibility and have robbed self of the fluid of spirit that flows as universal energy.

Is it any wonder the body dries up and decays?

Fill yourself with His presence.

Let His vitality move through you, as you. Catch the song of the Psalmist who sang to his Lord in this manner, "When I consider Thy heavens, the work of Thy fingers, the moon and the stars, which Thou hast ordained; What is man, that Thou art mindful of him? and the son of man, that Thou visitest him?" (Psalms 8:3-4)

Life, I ask you.

Tutor me in ways of understanding that the soul does not remember and has not yet learned.

My mind must remember or the path I have traveled serves little purpose.
Life's map not only delineates the route of the journey but the destination and plan of return.
Life, I am ready, I am receptive, and I am responsive to your instruction.
I no longer resist that which you choose to send through me even though at times the pain seems more than I can bear.
I have shared experiences with many people in life's school.
They have hurt in not knowing life is a distribution center of understanding.

Life, I accept your strength as my own and move forward under your vitality and guidance.
I recall the Psalm: "When Thou saidst, Seek ye my face; my heart said unto Thee, Thy face, Lord, will I seek." (Psalms 27:8)

Teach me, Oh, greatest of teachers.
Hold me in the womb of Your mind, that I too, might share in the conceiving of ideas and give birth to You as the truth of my being.
Let Yourself be made manifest through me as I open my being to let You flow through me.
I know Your law and strive to be obedient to it.
This You said, "Of every tree of the garden thou mayest freely eat: But of the tree of the

knowledge of good and evil, thou shalt not eat of it: for in the day that thou eatest thereof thou shalt surely die." (Genesis 2:16-17)

Man in ignorance and disobedience to this law has given power to disease, unhappiness, lack, and death through his dual nature.

The freedom of choice has been given to man, and it must be guided by wisdom and supported by love.

In our transgression of this law, death comes to free the spirit so that it may renew itself and prepare for a new body.

Then, again, it will take up the search for understanding.

The law does not change; it stands absolute, rendering total justice.

Teach me well.

Life has gorged herself at the feast of information but I stand ready for pure instruction.

I am Your pupil.

Remember, I am a product of Your thoughts and made after the image of Yourself and like You in all ways.

Help me to realize this truth.

You, great universe, are my mother and father.

I stand now, naked, ready to be clothed in your eternal truth. I am willing to shed the coat of man colors of understanding and step into the seamless robe of pure truth.

Yes, prepare me to wear the garment of Christ, "The Seamless Robe."

I wait in silence, no longer mesmerized by man's world.

The fields of competition are for those struggling with self, who are afraid, unsure and insecure.

Like in the Parable of the Rich Fool, man prepares, only to be lost in the preparation.

Richness of living is in the present tense—not something to be put off.

Self-preservation is folly, for we must learn the truth: self is indestructible spirit substance perfecting its own cause.

Gradually, we are seeing the flaws in man's world.

Yes, I am aware of his unscrupulous methods and cagey techniques.

The carving knife of ambition cuts a sharp edge but dulls with time and is worn thin to breaking.

Let it not be so with me, life.

Hear me, life, I beg you, hear me!

The journey has been long and traveling informative.

We are all world travelers in spirit, and life has given generously of herself.

Follow My pattern, You say, "Ask for light, seek illumination and use My ideas intelligently. Have faith in yourself as My son thinking through you. Stir your imagination into activity and see that which I have established for your welfare. Be not afraid of your dreams, for they are My dreams. Through you, I will establish My kingdom and peace shall endure because you have learned to be peaceful. Did you not hear the angels' message, hundreds of years ago, when they proclaimed to a sleeping world, 'Peace on Earth, good will toward man?'"

Yes, I was there.

Faintly, I heard the message.

Yet, in traveling too fast, we forget.

"Take time, son, to remember. Take time to listen. Take time to realize Me. Take time!"

I now remember.

I have always been with You, God, and have my true existence in Your eternalness—yes, in the realm of Your own Mind.

I have been alerted to the fact: I have been here since time began—since the foundation of the world.

Yes, Teacher, my soul does remember.

* * *

You say, "Was it yesterday?"

God once said that a day is like a thousand years and a thousand years like one day.

Why then should time be one of our concerns?

Just what is time?

Some have tried to define it but are unable to give a suitable definition.

Events have been recorded to justify man's

growth and evolvement as he passes through the stages of reincarnation.

The world presents a list of chronological happenings and calls them past civilizations.

These accounts have brought us to where we now stand.

Our calendar becomes a system by which man regulates his life.

It is a system of control and pushes man into a race against himself, building feelings of limitation.

Panic sets in as the push becomes greater and the race takes on a frantic, breathless pace.

The struggle for survival becomes a satire on living, for in truth man survives in spite of himself.

The calendar suggests a limited number of days broken up into weeks, divided into hours that melt into minutes which are the children of seconds.

Time effortlessly and relentlessly moves into years.

Time becomes a gauge by which man rushes into living but fails to grow.

With all this explosive pressing, man lives by a false concept and puts self in bondage to it.

Time is greater than weeks, months, or even years, for it is eternal.

* * *

There is talk about seasons, but what are they, but part of the whole?

Seasons are part of the plan and serve their purpose without making rash claims.

Seasons are made for man not man for the seasons.

*   *   *

From Genesis to Revelation, page by page, we have traveled.

We live in His garden of abundance; we have been put to tilling the soil from which we ourselves came and which one day will reclaim us.

We have walked with Patriarchs and with Prophets.

Yes, we have lived with kings, marched in vast armies, fought many battles,but self is the final battle.

Victory is within our reach. Grasp it!

*   *   *

The life of Jesus has always been very real and vivid to me.

Yes, I now remember, for I was there.

Throughout the territory, there were rumors of a new birth.

They say a star announced the event, but only a few received the message.

I heard them say, "He is an extraordinary

child, destined to be a king."

The news was whispered among the caravan travelers and sealed in the hearts of the shepherds, who silently accepted the new gift.

Wise men in their quest for truth followed after its rays.

A new dispensation had begun, and man yielded to the changing course of events.

Freedom from tradition and bondage from the past was no longer a dream.

A new light had come into the world, and the darkness was being dissipated.

* * *

A surge of freedom possessed me, no longer was I held by the Mosaic Law but now love was the supreme ruler.

Yes, a new law was being written on the heart of mankind, a new code of ethics for human behavior.

I can hear it yet—"A child is born. His name is love, and this is the new law."

The Christine era is my first clear remembrance as a soul expressing in a body. I remember so well how His light began to shorten the shadows in man's life.

* * *

I admit the mind can be colored by stories which cause mental vagueness.

Yet, I do remember.

Deep in my subconscious is a scene I have long remembered and only recently understood.

I have been challenged on hearing others report it from what they have read.

No, it was not a pleasant scene.

It shocked my emotional nature and imbedded fear.

I have learned fear strangles the life of man, and fear must die so man can live!

Death is a prison that must be cleansed to become the Temple of the living God.

Only then is man resurrected into life eternal.

Man can become a prisoner of karma until he breaks the shackles of bondage and declares his freedom.

Have ye not heard?

"Ye shall know the truth, and the truth shall set you free."

Yes, free from even karma as you cross out error and enter into conscious oneness with your creator.

* * *

Lifetime after lifetime, the scene stands as a monument to life not death.

I am reminded constantly that life is continuous, and there is continuity in its progressive movement.

Many of us remain where we are for we stand at an empty cross, bewildered and lost.

Tears cloud our eyes; we are unable to see either the empty cross or the hollow tomb.

Christ lives! I tell you!

Christ lives as the very substance of self, waiting to be recognized, eager to be acknowledged.

The search continues.

Christ must live in man as man.

He is more than an intellectual knowing.

He is a Divine Presence and the central figure of every person.

I am sure I knew Jesus.

I was in His Presence.

I am sure I heard Him speak, not once, but many times.

He was the wayshower, for He turned man from self to the Father within.

He never made any personal claims for the man Jesus but gave credit where it belonged.

He admitted He could function only as the Divine Principle flowed through Him.

He was unable to perform any thing of Himself but able only by the Infinite Power that is God.

Days before the experience that shocked me deeply and still draws tears, I was fascinated by the exhilaration of activity.

There was a commercial excitement that filled the air like burning incense.

Taxes must be paid, and people needed housing.

The odor of spices and food cooking filled the narrow streets—teasing the sense of smell.

Even the uninteresting streets were now peopled with the royal garments of pageantry in color.

Soldiers manned their prancing mounts and rode arrogantly about shouting orders.

A constant stream of rags and riches mingled and mixed.

Garments, intricately woven of fine imported fabric splashed with vibrant color, added life to the dull drab cloak of the beggar and leper.

I was more interested in the faces and studied them deeply.

There were those who walked as in a trance, lifeless and dusty from travel, wearing a weariness that belonged to a complicated system of what is called survival.

Life had whipped many until their flesh was wrinkled from its beatings.

There were eyes dull from bitterness, others bright and dancing, and those that registered no meaningful expression at all.

This picture seems to depict the whole human race and retells itself in every city of our land.

All persons were concerned with the man Jesus for he was on trial for His life.

His frankness and honesty were exemplary.

The Sanhedrin greatly feared Jesus for this meant exposure of their own deceit.

Pilate, unable to make a decision that would jeopardize his own throne, was a coward.

However, the people eagerly awaited Pilate's decision, anticipating the worst.

To me, it was a sordid and flimsy drama cast in the life of an innocent man.

Even I had to question: was this a form of shock therapy to a weary worn world, torn between tradition and devotion?

With all my feelings, I remained as much apart from the scene as possible.

Soon the time for the formal announcement came, and the final decree was to be spoken.

I was interested to find Pilate could not speak against Jesus but released the decision into the hands of the masses.

I knew he was freeing his own consciousness of a debt to love.

The stimulus of anger-fired prejudice brought cries from the people.

I can hear them yet, "Not Jesus Barabbas, but Jesus who claims to be the Christ!"

So it was, mob law was the scēne not a hall of justice.

In the twinkling of an eye, I realized a journey

into eternity had begun.

I was consciously aware of the tremendous lessons being taught.

I stood in awe of this man who could stand silent before His accusers.

He was fearless for He knew His destiny was not the cross but total acceptance into Infinite Mind.

I watched Him as He stood, tall in stature, poised and confident—the Master Teacher, a craftsman schooled in shaping and molding human lives.

Yes, a MAN among men; a man who had actually put God into every experience of life.

He tried to deliver His message helping man to realize his divinity.

He spent hours healing the sick, comforting the grief-stricken, and teaching, teaching, teaching.

This I said is a man. Yes, He is truly the Son of God!

* * *

My soul assured me this was an expedition into a great discovery for real identity.

In this moment, I knew one body could never tell the story, but many bodies are required for life's lessons.

We must live in the body of many personalities, wear different colors and change sex in order to make the final adjustment.

What man calls death is but transition from life to life.

Mother Earth endows man with a body as her gift to life; this is the laboratory in which man experiments and seeks to prove identity.

What we call death is release from personal to the universal, "The Law of Expansion."

The journey Jesus traveled is not unlike the one you and I take.

His journey was not simply a type of experiment to prove a formula, but it was a formula that gave proof to the experiment.

Jesus shows us life equals life and that death is a catalyst which moves us from one expression to another.

The last enemy to be conquered is the fear of death, not death, for it is fear that starves the spirit in the body.

Try to picture the mental process that was now taking place in Jesus as the shadow of the cross stood before Him.

Death held no vain imaginings for life was His answer.

Once more, we return to the scene and the hum of activity, watching the curiosity seekers, people numb with fright, others filled with a frenzied fever of hate propelled by pride and lust for power.

There were those so engrossed in sorrow; the pain shook their bodies.

Yes, others were too troubled in thought to utter even casual greetings.

Tears streamed down pale faces, tense and filled with anguish.

Some were repelled by the moment, too shocked to look upon the scene, but followed, caught up in the crowd of temperament and mixed emotions.

My soul remembers, for it was a fearful moment.

* * *

I stood beyond the crowd unable to see the face of Jesus, the man being sent to His death, but my body relaxed as a strong vibration engulfed me.

I responded to His Presence and felt His power deep within my own body temple.

The end of His journey brought strange sounds as the wooden cross was pulled over stone and gravel streets.

I could feel the movement and pain in my own body.

Pain came as a sensation unique to suffering yet with a reward in its painfulness.

It was the kind of pain that awakens an inner stirring and annoints the body with cleansing.

The sounds with their studied tempo were mysteriously haunting.

Suddenly, I was unable to control the tears that flowed over my face.

I sensed a deep loss and felt inadequate to help in any way; I could only watch and send Him a special brand of love, that which He Himself had taught.

I remember the woman who barely touched the fringe of His garment and received her healing.

What a moment this must have been in her life—to touch the very heart of the Infinite.

How close I was, yet how far away.

What was it that stood between me and this man?

Only my eyes followed the marching procession to the hill; my ears were attuned to the mysterious sounds.

I heard it then.

I hear it now.

Could it be the same mob, confused, torn between self and God?

* * *

Like rehearsed actors, their shouts rang and echoed, "Kill Him! Kill Him!"

A mental sedative seemed to come over the people as the cross was raised.

A quietness brought an exchange of words as Jesus gave His final lesson on forgiveness.

Jesus released Himself to God and freed man to work out his own salvation.

I tell you the cry is still heard in our land as

people weep, wonder, and are confused, hungry and afraid.

Yes, I live with it now, and my soul remembers when!

The hill became obscure in my tear-clouded eyes, and the three crosses blended into one.

I could look no longer but turned away; I do not recall leaving the hill.

In memory, I see only an empty cross.

I questioned.

"Is this the man destined to live in unity with God and man throughout eternity as the eternal message of peace and love?"

This is the man.

Now, I realized it.

How much growing was required of Jesus to reach this point and how long must man live to come into a realization of this truth?

Only life has the answers.

* * *

What man calls death came to my body rather suddenly, and the soul quickly decided to find another environment in which to express and grow.

I am not sure as to the lapse of time between incarnations, but it was relatively short.

Life carried me to a strangely enchanting land,

totally different from my previous life.

It was a land of rigid customs.

The people moved with quick steps yet stood still in the face of tradition.

The way of life was leisurely, but there was a flare of elegance that found expression through simplicity in lines and contours that were fluid with emphasis on preserved beauty.

The philosophy of the people had a tone of similiarity with what Jesus taught.

Buddha was the God.

Buddha spoke with great wisdom, bringing a breath of freshness to the lifeless words.

I learned much from this oriental teaching, and it has endured through many generations for it is woven into the very warp and woof of the Christian world.

Today, a glazed Buddha stands in my home because of a memory.

This Buddha is a happy image and sits in retired contentment, holding in his hollow interior the names of people with whom I keep a vigil of prayer.

My body was that of a slight man, highly animated with energy.

For the most part, my life was uneventful and reasonably short.

I spent much time among the delicate blossoms of the garden, beside quiet pools, reflecting on life and her purpose.

In our peaceful home, I shared life with a love that could not last for numerous reasons.

Class distinction brought much difficulty to love that did not recognize man's differences.

Life without her would not have been life, but because of this both our lives ended by my hand.

This I wish my soul did not remember.

In life's lessons, I have learned nothing is destroyed.

There are times when it must be removed in order to build again—to build a finer structure, a new skyline—to raise the vision, to create a new image.

The old must make way for something more durable and more beautiful.

So it was, and the Master Sculpturer was already chiseling on a new piece of His handiwork.

* * *

My soul craved excitement and love, so it migrated to another oriental country and placed me in the body of what was to become one of China's most popular geishas.

My temperament and body had a flare for the artistic; I was moved to create.

Hand painting was only one of the arts in which I engaged.

For the most part, my life was taken up by my work as a geisha.

Time was spent catering to the needs of many, leaving my own soul unfed and hungry.

Everything within me hungered for life and a fuller expression of it.

It was my desire to share with one man rather than have my body as a crossroad for many.

Inwardly, this starvation brought illness, and once more I brought destruction to the body through suicide.

Suicide is a most unfortunate way to leave the body for there is much confusion and great distress.

Even in spirit, I wandered helplessly for a long period of time trying to regain conscious awareness of my true nature.

I only remembered that I was Tonya and Tonya was no more.

Tonya had been a personality and had died with the flesh.

* * *

Once more the soul, asking for another opportunity, sought a new experience.

I reveled in the thought of living again and taking up a new body for the sake of joy and gaiety.

I realized there was a definite bitterness in me that had to be overcome because of past experiences.

This time, I wanted only to charm, taunt and tease.

There was a wildness to my spirit that was

almost uncontrollable.

I arrived in one of the lower European countries.

Here my feet whirled to gypsy music.

Love was the order of the day, much love, more than I had yet experienced.

There was not just one man in my life but men, men, men!

Everywhere I went, music beat its rhythm of fast living.

Music was in the streets, in the market places.

Yes, music was even there as we indulged in each other.

My body was a restless bundle of explosive energy; sculptured and trim.

My wild beauty caught the eye of a Pasha who purchased me as his personal concubine.

I let myself be bought for it gave me a recognized position.

I no longer was a nobody of the streets.

In spite of this, I remained more empty than ever before.

A strange loneliness attached itself to me with a passion.

I could not shake it or find freedom from a feeling of desperation.

Life had become a series of demands, requests and harsh orders.

I had been bought for a price; I had sold myself to lose myself.

Panic drove me into the streets, back to the

men I entertained in dreams.

Once more I threw myself into the currents of the sense world.

Once more, I was caught up with undisciplined feelings and gave full vent to every emotion.

These men had nothing to give but themselves, for jewels were not a part of their price.

Their need was only to use, to take, to leave, to come back and take again.

My only comfort was in their taking.

They spoke kindly, caressed and spent themselves fully.

The experience had no value but to make the body scream for more.

I became an addict to men and a slave to their ruthless habits.

The body which had been a vessel of desire now became a curse; I tell you, she was a raging tyrant.

What once was pleasure now met with disgust, and I lived in a mental state of anguish and frustration.

I reached out to life to again answer me and clarify my needs.

My heart beat a pounding rhythm of pain, causing sleepless nights filled with remorse.

Feverish desire lurked in my world, leaving tracks of guilt, as life began to refine her action.

I was tortured and tormented beyond my ability to bear.

This drove me once more into the streets where I could forget in moments of ecstasy.

Fear working with jealousy put a blade through my heart; the pain I still remember.

The body had been evacuated.

Again, I was free to ponder my experiences.

* * *

Life, I ask you.

Bring peace to my troubled soul.

I am weary worn and know not the direction to take.

Give me yourself that I might live and learn on a higher plane.

If I be lifted up by your energy then I can light myself into new understanding.

* * *

Into the melting pot of life, I once more was being refined to be poured into a mold ready for a more fruitful experience.

Life had expressed in many bodies and in many loves since that eventful experience on the hill.

Help me to remember the message, the deep teachings that poured from His gentle lips.

Reveal truth to me as it was revealed at the empty tomb.

Let me, too, know the truth that lives eternal and sets man free from the self and personality that binds and constricts.

Let me know the humility that He possessed and the ability to live by it.

I am unsure and feel strange in my new world to which you have sent me.

For years men have considered this a dark continent, and this is where you desire to teach me.

I, like Him, must say, "Your will be done, not mine."

I accept it as another of life's lessons on the pathway back to the original source.

I realize you are in the process of teaching and grooming me for my contribution.

You say, I must learn tolerance; I must get more understanding and learn these things well.

I come into this present world foreign to its ways and its people; I am an alien.

In this life, my world is a mass of brown, black and copper bodies.

I, too, accept my new garment of flesh and will make every effort to wear it well.

The great universe is now teaching me my next important lesson in her graduated school of life.

Inspiration began to fill me, and I felt a power that was generating a new kind of experience.

Slowly, God was releasing a form of prayer through me; primitive, yes, but it was definitely prayer.

I found myself alone much of the time in a sort of meditation that one cannot explain.

Devotion was more than words and acts.

Devotion was a deep inner realization that something greater than myself was guiding, directing, and moving me into an expanded consciousness.

My feelings did not speak for the others, for the power I was feeling seemed unknown to most of our people.

Once more, the pageant of the cross moved through my mind; He lives, some how I know He lives.

The cross lost its sorrow, and I rejoiced in the knowledge I was beyond that experience.

Yes, God was blessing my ebony temple in wonderous ways as He made His Presence felt in me.

Presently, I felt that I had found a part of myself long lost, and here it was.

I am speaking of the real self, not that which appears to be.

I was beginning to like my new experience, and Africa was home to me at last.

My pioneering spirit finally found a degree of rest in this new adventure.

Yes, it was an exploration in the pages of eternity.

Life was good to me, for she gave me the love of a quiet yet mentally alert partner.

He was handsome and possessed a strength

not disguised by muscle.

Time after time, he would question me saying, "Who are you? Where have you been?"

Explanation at this point was impossible, for neither of us knew the answers.

We could only believe, trust, and know that there was a plan bigger than either of us.

He reminded me often that I was different from the others, haughty yet with a softness; a product of many mixed emotions.

We felt very much together, but yet, there was a separateness one cannot explain.

He would say over and over, "You are mine, I love you. Yet, I do not have you completely."

His kindness was God's gentleness being expressed through him.

I desired him above all else in my life, for such love I had never tasted.

His body was like my own, a blending that brought total compatibility.

Our love was endorsed with deep feelings; everything within us embraced this union.

Our God became real to us in our own special way, although He remained far removed to many.

In silence, we sought Him, while others chanted or used frantic gyrations of the body to induce His favor.

True, this method of prayer still holds many in bondage to a past they remember and cannot forget.

For many, this past is their present, and they have no future since they are bound by habitual patterns.

We were happy to be free.

* * *

How clearly I recall his chiseled face showing approval while blazes from the fire leaped and played on the ground like happy children.

His clear eyes told me much that could not be revealed even in speaking.

Yes, my soul remembers.

Yes, how well, it remembers.

At last, I had learned one of life's precious lessons: a lesson in human love.

Love is almost impossible to define, for in defining there are limitations.

Let me say, it is a feeling like none other.

It is that which would cause you to leave all else and follow its path.

It is deep, moving, penetrating, and charges the cells of the body with vitality and a sense of quiet joy.

One does not talk about love promiscuously.

Love is a sacred gift, a gift received without wrappings or obligation.

In love, one gives the whole self in order to receive more of life's gift.

One must never violate this gift, because it is in stealing the soul is robbed of its richness.

One cannot take that which is joined with another and expect joy.

Joy is not the reward of a thief.

Our love unified us as one unit, seeking only to satisfy itself in each other.

There was never a reaching out to other lives.

Our love was a love confined to our own souls.

You ask about love and tell me it hurts.

This is true, but in its hurting there is healing.

In its pain there is sudden joy that releases all sense of memory of pain.

Love is a balm that soothes anything that would bring injury to it.

Love does not ask but stands ready to give of itself to better serve self.

This kind of love I have known; this was our love—a very special love.

Even heights of passion knew tenderness and brought a subdued quietness in its richest moments.

Moments alone, my soul remembers how my body ached and hungered for his closeness.

The warmth and softness of his flesh was like the cloak of prayer itself.

In his nearness, I could not remember any separation.

Our love lived, it was vital and inspired, bringing fulfillment to all our needs and desires.

His hands were my guide.

His love was my strength.

His tears; they became my humility.

"Why could not such a love bring forth children?" you ask.

What about children?

They are only life seeking itself.

We had our own adjustments and were too busily engaged in growing.

All energy was needed for our own purposes.

I was concerned, however, that my body had not been able to bear or be blessed by giving life.

At times I felt barren—an empty vessel that could not be filled.

In quietness, I asked life to use my body, to let an idea be born through it.

I offered myself as a source of re-entry into the physical world for some other soul in search.

In spite of our love, there was a feeling within me that longed to feel the pulsations of life and growth.

Yes, to know the pain of birth and the joy of giving.

I even wanted to wrestle with the pain in order to hear life cry its way back.

I found that this was not my mission or my task.

I could only rest in the love I had.

Rather quickly, a tiredness crept over my body like the clouds closing out the rays of the sun.

I felt strange and had a feeling of being under some sort of natural sedation.

Try as I did to persuade life, she would not extend herself to me in this body.

Her course had been run, and she no longer felt it necessary to maintain this temple.

She had spent her energy, served her purpose, and now must return to the giver.

So few years, yet a lifetime of love had been squeezed into thirty-odd years of growing.

Another span had been added to the bridge of life, and its name was love.

My only regret was leaving the man who had given me more than many lifetimes.

I loved him, and the pain of separation was unbearable.

The struggle in consciousness had begun, but again life was the winner.

I quietly passed from the earth plane, knowing I had drunk from life's richest nectar, LOVE!

My soul lingered in the area trying to bring peace to the love I left.

I made every effort to reinforce his grief with the love we had both known and shared.

Hours I remained at his side, praying, as his ebony face washed itself in a profusion of tears.

"Know I am with you," I would say, and

there were times I believed he knew.

He would become quiet and clutch the grass pillow to his face as though it were my own.

Days passed, and I requested life to let him join me.

Life was good and granted him freedom from a grief-stricken body.

* * *

I was soon being drawn to a new experience quite remote from the former ones.

Due to my former experience, I was pulled to a deeply religious family steeped in tradition and hours of ritual.

At an early age, they placed me in a convent for training.

I was struck with fear, a fear that almost caused madness.

The discipline was strict, and the hours were long.

A combination of work and controlled prayer became a way of life.

We lost contact with the outside world and the affairs of state.

With all the prompting, I was able to take my final vows and become a nun.

In spite of my vows, there was much I resisted and was cautioned by the superiors that God would punish me for this type of disobedience.

I was not afraid of my God, but I was afraid

of my superiors.

The routine of prayer was so mechanical that it became monotonous.

I refused to take part in it but prayed within myself according to the promptings of my own indwelling Lord.

Much was seen over the edges of the prayer book as God was sending His message through my heart.

Time takes care of all things, and so it was with me.

A call was received for a missionary sister, and I responded to this call.

I had been trained in the care of emotionally and mentally disturbed minds.

This gave me a deeper insight into the human being and taught me why the body is compelled to suffer for lack of mental discipline.

The boat trip was long but afforded me a freedom I had not enjoyed since childhood.

The great ocean seemed so much a part of me as we tossed in the waves frosted by her vigor.

I loved her as she slapped the hull and stern of our ship.

I felt her strength as she beat upon rocks and sand.

This was a new experience — a new friend.

We arrived in South America; the headquarters were in Peru.

We were escorted by carriage to a high point beyond the crowded city where the convent was located.

The Superior appeared to be a harsh woman, but, behind her armor of protection, she carried an abiding love for the Christ.

We became inseparable friends, taking long walks together and confiding in each other.

We especially enjoyed the gardens that were carefully tended by Juan, our all-around-man.

In our times together, we would discuss many matters and our relationship to them.

We are too confined she would say; some day it will be different.

We are too cut-off from the real world to render any great service.

I agreed and confessed my desire to serve life through prayer activity.

Both of us felt prayer had its rightful place, but agreed it calls the hands and feet to action.

Prayer without works is dead.

The cloistered life did not stop me from reaching out in thought to the world that lay beyond the great walls.

I knew that one day I would enter that world.

The walls were not my boundaries; they could not confine me.

Straight they stood like giant sentinels in our world.

Yes, there is so much I remember, my soul does not forget.

My life had a richness and, for the time, I was satisfied being married to God.

The marriage was heaven-ordained they told us, yet I remained very much a part of the earth and subject to human desires.

The chalk white habits sang their song, flowing from our bodies and sweeping over the stone walks.

Our black ones brought somberness and reverence to the dignity of our order.

I was always reaching for the crucifix to remind me of my obligations that otherwise slipped my mind.

I loved the smell of salt water as the spray sent a delightful aroma over our walls.

I enjoyed her manner of speech as she poured herself over the cliffs and the rocks below.

The heavy humidity gave us an abundance of vegetation.

Flowers blooming on all sides appeared as smiles in God's world.

I loved them and caressed their petals with tenderness.

Even in this world of solitude the atmosphere was alive with vibrant colors and great vitality.

Prayer, you ask about prayer.

What is prayer but man, living, being that which God created him to be.

Is not life the very prayer of God moving through man?

In our world, man is so accustomed to words, he tries to live through what he spits from his mouth.

Prayer is silent communion that builds an inner reserve for those periods of emergency.

Prayer is like a dam in human consciousness that directs the flow of infinite energy and gives direction to its movement.

It is a type of spiritual reservoir and needs mental engineering to operate at peak performance.

I call prayer heaven's conservation plan and program.

Now, I will tell you about prayers, for I remember vespers when the giant bells would swing high in the tower and send their call far across hillside and valley.

People are being called to prayers; it is time to worship.

Columns of black habits move in precision toward the chapel, and, as they go, one by one, in face-framing hoods, stiffly starched, projecting like blinders on either side, I watch until I, too, must fall in line.

With attention focused forward, we cannot be distracted by passing happenings.

I remember as they passed how deeply I felt for each one, knowing something of the loneliness each one felt.

Each face told a story, this I especially remember.

Yes, I, too, have my story.

A story that keeps me awake in the midnight of my life.

A story that tears at the heart like the waves beating the coastline below.

A story written by life and not by temporary enclosures.

Yes, life present, past, and life yet to come.

During my many walks in the garden I had taken special notice of Juan.

Frequently, I took liberty to talk with him and speak with gaiety, reflecting my inner feelings.

There was something in him that drew me to him in a way that brought fear to my mind.

I questioned, "What is it this man has to do with me? Why is it I feel this magnetic attraction that pulls me in its mighty current?"

My feelings were strong, shadowed by guilt, yet I was helpless in my effort to gain freedom from them.

This was wrong for a nun to entertain such feelings, yet they were present in me.

My path crossed his many times, and somehow he understood my intentions.

Now, ask me about love, for this is a type of love but not love itself.

Love is often cruel in its attempt to adjust itself and be lifted up.

The pain can be more severe than any physical illness.

Even in the hurting, there is a peculiar comfort.

Love is a feeling transmitted between souls that remember and long once more to find solace in union.

These souls forget careless use of energy brings destruction.

Love, yes, I am speaking of love, not sex.

Man has been misinformed regarding both.

Man has come to believe that love is sex and has distorted the image.

In his confusion he misuses both, weeping in his so doing.

Energy is energy and can be directed into whatever channel the mind will send it.

Sex is an action resulting from a personal reaction.

The reaction itself proves to be unsatisfactory at times and brings violence rather than harmony.

We must guard ourselves against the wrong use of any power, for that power is redirected back to the sender with precise accuracy.

With all this knowing, the temptation was more than I could resist.

Consciously aware of my vows made years ago, time dulled the utterances I made.

Why is it we forget things we should remember?

My only concern now was that I needed Juan more than I needed vows or anything my present world could give me.

Shocked? Yes, I was shocked, but I was practical enough to be brutally honest.

Tell me, life, why does my soul remember?

This, too, my soul remembers: a hard pillow, wet with tears; long, dark nights in a lonesome cell whose interior boasted earthly possessions of a prayer book, candle, straw mattress, and crucifix.

The walls projected an unfriendly feeling with their stark coldness.

Bare, they stood, like a person stripped of possessions.

We were told this helped to keep our mind on God and spared us the desire to possess things.

I tell you; God did a better job in creating His world.

He did not fill it with drabness but adorned her with extravagant beauty.

Soon, I learned my feelings were the feelings of many of my Sisters.

More than a few were torn in the struggle between devotion and service.

Hard, gruelling work helped some to forget; temper was a release for others, while fear mocked the hearts of the timid ones.

I am grateful that some could reveal it as

joy and radiate His love sincerely and purely.
There were only a few, I tell you, not many.

I longed to go beyond those great walls and began to evolve a plan in which I could make this journey.

The world I had left behind was once more calling me, and I knew I must answer.

An urgent need for help among the poor was evident, and the numbers to serve were few.

Opportunity had presented herself to me; she beckoned, and I responded.

My request was granted on the basis that our gardener accompany me on these outings.

Now, life had given me more than I had bargained for; this new experience unlocked the huge carved wooden gates.

Outside lay a waiting world, tired, commercial, rushing, sick, pleading her case, and trying to find peace in her own unwillingness to yield.

I saw all manner of things, and I recalled that this is what an open door reveals.

My friend Juan, his donkey loaded with supplies, and myself wove our way up the hillside into the country area.

Here we ministered to the sick, the hopeless, and the confused.

These were a part of the world's unknowing victims.

They were not yet aware of a great truth

that would one day deliver them from this treadmill of habitual difficulty.

I loved them, as they reached out to me for light and love in their child-like ways.

The friendship between Juan and me grew deeper, and a strange emotion began to write her story.

There was untold anxiety that beat us both like lashing whips.

I remember an occasion, while resting near a small waterfall, that his arms caught me.

His velvet lips told what he had been unable to speak and had sealed in his heart.

I realized this was the soul of my former husband that followed me and now lived in Juan.

Once more we rested in the love we once shared.

It was only a moment, but it still lingers.

I was no longer afraid; I did not resist; I gave what I had to give.

Our eyes met often and spoke a language unknown to the others.

A clasp of the hand sent love wildly through our bodies to later rest in its converted energy.

Strange happenings were taking place in my body.

I was grateful the habit concealed much, but for how long could the concealment last?

In a terrifying moment, I realized this lifetime was soon to be ended.

I had transgressed the law, and to break the law is death to the body.

The law is an action unto itself, only we had set it in operation.

I rejoiced to know my body could yield a harvest, yet I knew I could not reap it.

Life became a state of constant fear.

Hell was claiming her victim, she had received her own.

I lived in this state with a burning conscience that brought me utter despair.

My only salvation was that I had Juan's love, and I seemed to carry the burden with lesser weight.

There was a torment within that shook my frame; yes, a rebellion that set my thoughts into whirling motion.

I ask, "Is it wrong to love? Is isolation more respected of God than honest love?"

No, God created us that we might love one another, but I am understanding this love must be qualified.

Love wears no price tag, it is a gift of the spirit.

The nights were darker and longer than usual.

I was growing weary in trying to find a way out.

Yes, I tell you, I was weary.

The moment of truth had come, and I knew I must do what I must do.

Quietly, I slipped from my room down the long uninviting corridor.

I pushed through the chapel doors and fell prostrate before the altar.

How long I was there, I do not remember; the crisis was over, and now I knelt in silent prayer.

"My Lord and my God,
You know my troubled heart.
And You know my body.
Accept my restless soul.

This act I must do,
Lord, you will forgive.
I must go through death
That I once more may live.

The prayer book is closed,
And the rosary said.
A candle lit.
Yes, Lord — A bowed head.

Take back my soul,
I ask You now.
Show me the way;
Lord, tell me how.

Oh, bless these lives
That I must leave behind.
Help them forget, Lord.
Let them be kind.

The child that I hold,
It, too, must go.
For it only came, Lord,
To rest my troubled soul.

These tears that I weep
They are not for me.
I ask for sleep, Lord,
Please let it be."

Slowly, I lifted my head to catch the glow of many candles.

Someone sat at the organ, although the bench was empty.

Music filled the chapel and drifted like fresh air around me.

The organ, too, has many moods.

Often, her notes are sad.

They are haunting, they tell of love, and quiver in their crying.

The peaceful message soothed me, but I needed to tear myself from her and finish what my mind told me I must do.

I paused at the Stations of the Cross long enough to remember the climb to Calvary.

The weight of the cross was heavy on my shoulders, and my heart grew faint.

Time was fleeting, and life was pushing.

The night welcomed me with a great expanse of twinkling lights.

The golden moon smiled sadly and slipped behind a cloud.

I picked up my pace and moved quickly

through the garden to the stairs along the wall.

As I approached the stairs, a figure emerged from the darkness and clutched me desperately.

"Juan," I cried.

He was tense and frightened.

"Juan, it is you."

Our embrace was one filled with indescribable terror; a moment of moments.

We knew this would be our last and in it declared a love that would endure forever as a tribute to itself.

Tears trickled over our burning lips and splashed in our laughter.

If only I could have died in his arms rather than take the step before me.

Words were not spoken.

A silent communication still lives in my memory.

Yes, oh, yes, how my soul does remember. I broke from his embrace and rushed up the cut-out stone stairs.

My eyes studied the rocks below and asked them to be kind in receiving me.

I once more heard the great ocean, in her relentless motion, shout with a conquering voice as her frantic waves tossed and lashed themselves upon the jagged ledges.

I heard the steps of Juan on the stair and knew that before he reached me, the plunge must be made.

In a frightful moment, as his hand reached for me, I found myself falling through space.

All the prayers I had ever said were repeated in that swift period of passing time.

I lived years in a few short seconds.

I could hear Juan's voice above the ocean, but there could be no returning.

Two bodies, one unborn and my own tormented temple, released their soul, as the rocks claimed their own.

The roaring tide continued to toss and foam.

The voice from the wall screamed into the night like a searching animal, lost and bewildered.

I can hear it yet.

"Wait for me. Look for me. I will find you, I will find you. Love like ours cannot be lost."

This life which united our souls in harmony will soon be teaching us in the next; the lessons we must learn in our need for body adjustment.

I was more aware of my life in the invisible world, although I found myself eager to return to the visible plane again.

Life had been complicated, and I had destroyed several bodies.

Now, I must return to one and cleanse the temple as a fit habitat for eternal goodness — God.

I must learn to have an appreciation for that which God endowed me.

I must learn to trust the body and know that it is mine to build by my own thinking process.

I must go into every corner and remove the

darkness, open the recesses of the subconscious and free the thoughts, begging for healing.

Yes, this I must do in order to obtain freedom.

During my time in the world of spirit, I gained new understanding and was better equipped to meed the demands of another incarnation.

I knew it would not be easy, but it must be done.

This time the early portion of my life was spent in Northern Europe, where I had all the advantages of culture.

I received instruction in the finest schools and was tutored by private teachers.

Life was beautiful, and I reaped the harvest of her planting.

With all her offerings, something in me looked to new horizons and freedom that I did not as yet know.

America, a new land, yes, America was calling me.

My family agreed if this were my desire they would furnish me with all the comforts within their power to give.

I accepted their generosity and started for a new land, a new life.

America is vast — a land of contrasts.

Her soil, a field of abundance, yielding to those who had the courage to enter into her willingness to supply.

She is a great country, making claims she often contradicts by her actions.

She, too, is a pupil and will learn her lessons as the individual citizen accepts his freedom.

America introduced me to her western states with the majestic mountains, placid lakes, and romping rivers.

Her great forests spoke of times I could only imagine as she whispered to the four winds.

I loved her and the purity of her untouched beauty.

America was my mother, and from her soil I wore her garment.

A garment of dust that one day I would shake from my real self but be the better for having worn it.

Life gave me a moody, thoughtful man, deliberate in his desire to make me an idol.

He worked tirelessly to give me what he thought I needed but never really awakened to my need.

He left me, never knowing my only need was to be needed.

We loved but with a detachment.

He could never quite let go of self long enough to give completely.

He was letting life push him rather than flow through him.

I did my best to be a comfort, meeting his needs to the best of my understanding.

Conception took place many times in my body, but none of the souls grew into maturity.

This was a cross not easy to bear, for I desired so deeply to give life to life.

I seemed to be a house through which souls passed as they were making a quick journey through life.

Sorrow gave birth to more sorrow, and six lives moved through me leaving the house empty.

My husband began to show the strain of toil and the drain of grief.

My life became a mental crutch upon which he walked and not lightly.

It was difficult to see him wear away.

Finally, life recalled him, and he left me to face the years alone.

I felt life had deserted me, and I was bitter, revengeful, and filled with self-pity.

I indulged in pretense, only to find life has a way of exposing even the most clever.

Life reimbursed me by sending into my experience a young homeless lad who became my son, by life giving to life.

Through him, God blessed my world, and the years passed with increased contentment.

There was a resurrected joy in me that began to shine forth, healing all the hurts and erasing names from tombstones.

This I was grateful for, knowing man is not of the earth but of heaven.

Tombstones are a market for unknowing people swayed by the race consciousness and in bondage to beliefs in destruction.

I tell you we are indestructible.

Yes, thank God, my soul remembers.

You ask about my world now?

I tell you, it is made up of memories of the past.

I am a composite of all the lives I have ever lived.

You have asked about a world.

There is no world.

There is only God.

We are part of His plan, possessing nothing yet, in trying to claim it, losing our way.

Man has a tendency to put labels on things and is involved in semantic confusion.

What about me today?

I can tell you, but I will not tell all.

What we look upon is only the reflection of our own thoughts. Time in her progressive movement changes even that.

Life is the mirror of the universe reflecting the patterns man holds for himself.

True, we are hesitant to give up our bodies for fear we shall lose identity.

Identity is only found when we are no longer submerged in personality and confused by the complex information revealed by the senses.

One day we shall know ourselves for what we are — indestructible spirit substance.

We shall know we are the temple of the living God and that we are eternal in the heavens, that ours is a temple not made with hands.

We are reminded of this in Corinthians 5:1: "For we know that if our earthly house of this tabernacle were dissolved, we have a building from God, not made with hands, eternal in the heavens."

Just as Jesus prayed in Gethsemane alone, deserted by weary disciples; we must go apart from the body in order to live.

The body serves as a prison where man is held until he proves his freedom.

We live in a body to learn order and gain spiritual momentum for new experiences.

Through experience and our natural resources we prove the validity of universal principle.

Again, you question me regarding my life now.

As I said, dare I tell you?

Could you understand, and would you be able to accept the truth as I know it?

There are some things the world is not ready for, but preparation is being made.

She must receive the truth or meet her destruction.

You have listened to race consciousness so long that you are mesmerized by it.

Your thinking is colored by what you see and influenced by what you hear.

You ask me regarding my struggles and success.

I have had both in varying degrees.

I wonder at times why it is so important to concern ourselves with our struggles when we have reached the pinnacle of success.

Is it not true that our struggles drove us toward perfect unfoldment?

Success is a word, a term and bears personal interpretation.

Success cannot be measured by another man's life but by your own spiritual yardstick.

Success is only a successive group of events that give one outer security, often depriving the soul of any great growth.

True success is built into consciousness and bears an outer security by its own efforts.

Consciousness is a stable foundation on which to build enduring success, for it is in consciousness that success is maintained and sustained.

I keep remembering all the things that have happened to me have been for my total understanding.

God knows this is a lesson far too difficult for the average wayfarer.

This requires a mental integrity beyond human effort.

Finally, I know that as God injects His life in me I become an animated being, expressing all that He is and all He would have me express in His world.

Man through the process of reincarnation has had the opportunity to increase and multiply his good through understanding of the righteous use of Infinite Law.

For some of us, the search goes on half-heartedly; for others, it is a serious business.

We all have our moments.

In our present generation, many barriers are being lifted, and walls of prejudice are falling.

Yes, the walls are crumbling, just as Jericho had to fall in order to be built up again.

I see it.

Yes, dear ones, the Kingdom of God is at hand.

Do you not see it?

Life has taught me certain freedoms, yet she has put me in bondage to things I have yet to learn, in the process of realizing wholeness.

Much of my growth has been withheld be-because society has a set of formulas to live by, and I cannot conform, nor will I.

The truth must be known: the shell must be broken.

Man is caught in a web woven by his own thinking.

Man is confused by sex, survival, and a personal ego in trying to be king.

When King Ego rules the body, man is

bound for destruction.

The armies of envy, jealousy, greed, pride, and arrogance move in to take over, and the King is dethroned.

May I ask you?

Is a man a man because he wears a body so interpreted as such?

If you cannot answer this, then you do not know the truth and must seek further understanding.

We are neither male nor female, but made in the image of love. We bear the likeness of love in all ways.

Is not the body a disguise for the soul?

Is not the flesh a mask that hides the real man?

Man is a perfect idea in the process of realization.

Few of us have ever seen man; we have only seen the garment he wears.

We are unable to get past the wall of flesh, for we have become enmeshed in it.

We must see man as he was created or wars will continue to plague our world, and destruction will come.

Jesus spoke a great truth yet to be understood, when He said, "He that hath seen me hath seen the Father." (John 14:9)

John referred to the man Jesus but emphasized the reflected glory that came through His teachings.

In fact, Jesus found it necessary to go away

in order for man to find himself and the Father.

The man Jesus did not want to stand in the way of man's coming into conscious awareness of his own divinity.

The Christ cannot be seen until personality is converted to light and love.

There is a new teacher in our land today.

It is the spirit of truth revealing itself to all receptive minds eager and ready for its message.

Yes, the road we have traveled has been long, at times the incline steep: through the desert of emptiness with its haunting beauty into the valleys of forgetting, we have risen to the mountain of realization.

The miles have been like footprints in sand, lost in the eternal motion of change, swept by the winds of imagination and challenged by the nothingness of time.

The soul has migrated to different lands seeking experience.

Personality has spoken in different tongues.

Yes, the road is a long road.

Once more, we stand on the threshold of eternity—waiting, asking, praying.

Once again, the eyes are dimmed by human tears as the search for understanding sets the soul to flight on another journey.

Even the soul is shaken by the selfish

motives of man and is hesitant to be committed to living again in the body.

Yes, even in our time with all our knowing, people still live in a world removed from truth.

Introspection tells us we must return.

We must free the world from its bondage to lies through the reformation of thought.

Lies live in cowards, who are tortured and tormented by the fear of exposure.

Exposure is freedom!

Tears, yes, they still flow from the hungry hearts of men and women.

Tears In the frantic search for an abiding love, we have let passion with its unhappiness drive her wedge of ugliness into the path of love.

Within the tear-drop is contained the cleansing fluid of the soul.

Be not ashamed of your tears, they spring from the wells of joy.

Tears are as molten substance flowing from the volcano of the soul as it sets the emotions free.

Tears erupt as cleansing, leaving a fertile bed for renewed understanding.

Grief is the failure to recognize the eternal.

Grief Grief stands as a ghost in man's life and robs him of joy. Grief remains a problem child until disciplined and instructed.

Let not the icy fingers of grief clutch you but

warm them with your own love.

The scale of life is balanced by equal portions of love as the intellect (male) and feeling (female) join in marriage.

Love Love has been in bondage to race consciousness and sat at the table of the senses feeding lavishly, only to feel a gnawing starvation within.

The physical appetite is a cannibal that eats of itself.

Yes, the body, finding little satisfaction with a temporal supply, cries for food.

Man's real hunger is a soul-hunger—a hunger to share, a hunger to love, a hunger for truth.

Only by truth will we be fed and nourished with her infinite supply.

Day by day, life is teaching her lessons in the classroom of experience.

More and more is being revealed, can you hear?

LISTEN . . .!

We must learn to trust in love.

In viewing her through the prism of life, we see the many facets of expression.

Love will produce the good you are seeking, for her desire is to fulfill herself.

God is love, and love demands order.

Order obliterates confusion and puts man on a stable foundation supported by love.

Love is writing her lessons on the tablets of

time and engraving on the consciousness of man the eternal truth of his being.

Do you feel love as she writes?

Can you accept love's message?

Love will direct us into a new dimension of thought.

Here the soul will receive revelation.

Together, let us kneel at the table of communion and absorb truth.

Let us take truth into our being and appropriate her into the living temple as life, joy, wholeness, abundance, and love.

Is a man a Negro because he wears a somber garment?

Brotherhood

Is not the life in him the same life you and I feel as the animation of our bodies?

Does not his heart beat with the same love that keeps ours in motion?

Is he not the image of God?

Is he not like God in all ways?

Do flowers show prejudice in their growing?

Does the red rose turn from the yellow blossom?

Color disturbs man, but God is not concerned.

For God, Love, is no respecter of persons, but God causes the sun to shine on the just and the unjust.

Let us not trouble our thoughts with color but concern ourselves with God's ideas.

As we look into the many faces, let us recognize God—God in unique expressions.

Is a man foreign because he was born in another area of the world?

Location does not make man an alien.

Do you not believe we are one with God?

If we are one with God then we are one with all creation.

If we do not believe this then we build a wall of separation that must fall inevitably.

Possessions, what are they?

Possessions A price paid for impressions. Has the generous giver of life made you proud or grateful?

Have possessions brought you happiness or are you in bondage to their safety?

Accept them for their use but do not cling to them for they will return your bondage.

Cling not to that which you must leave but instead build a richness of spirit.

Credentials for heaven are in consciousness.

Vanity is the peacock of the ego, spreading pride in a display of self-gratification.

Vanity Vanity walks in arrogance with a haughty stride.

Vanity, admired for short periods, becomes weary with over-indulgence.

Vanity is an injection of fear shot into the veins of human pride.

Vanity is a child of indifference lost in the

world of make-believe.

Paul in writing to the Philippians said in Chapter 2, verse 3: "Let nothing be done through strife or vainglory; but in lowliness of mind let each esteem other better than themselves."

Love, why do we question her?
Love gives herself without question.
Love It is only we who do not recognize her.

Love's message pours through man as a powerful influence.

The energy generated requires careful direction, or love becomes an explosive power to destroy.

Hate is the reverse action of this all-powerful faculty.

Hate is a child of confusion, a belief that needs lifting.

Hate is unredeemed love.

Human love travels the path of extremes and when blinded by foolishness becomes a clown of deception.

Love will lift our world.

Love will transform our world.

Love will balance our world on the axis of harmony with all life.

Love makes no harsh demands or complicated requests upon what it loves but *loves* — for this is its sole purpose.

Rest your head and heart in the bosom of love.

Love will give you comfort, and in her you will find peace.

Love has washed you in the rivers of understanding.

Love has dried you with her own warmth.

Love has washed away the hurts with her tears as they flowed with your own.

Love has sat with you in sadness, saying, "Come into the light of love and into the sunshine of gladness."

Love has opened doors which only her keys will unlock.

Let us ask forgiveness for the times we have flaunted her only to see her mutilated by some person afraid of love's honest approach.

Yes, my soul remembers love, and the moment of truth is a fearful moment for one not equipped to meet it.

Love moves in the arena of life, ready for the game of living.

Love accepts the challenge of growing.

Love is a precious gift.

Lovers seek counsel in courting love's way.

Love, as Jesus explained, does not cast self before the swine of human thought with man's tendency for indulgence.

Love moves through the corridors of time as a gracious witness to all humanity.

Love requires no analytical reasoning, for love is her own reason.

Love's shy partner is loneliness.

Loneliness is the understudy in the unfolding

drama of the soul.

The wardrobe of loneliness is shrouded by mystery, and loneliness lives in the tattered garment of anticipation.

Fear is her seamstress.

Loneliness is the ill-fitted garment which only love can adjust.

Emerge through the curtains of loneliness and step into the role God created you to play!

Laugh with the world!

Sing with her choir!

Drink in her beauty!

Free yourself from the long shadow that fear casts.

Take courage!

Make the first step and watch the shadows disappear as you stand in the great light of truth.

Money is a gambler's dream, a poor man's vision, a fool's price but a wise man's obedient servant.

Money

For many, money is their God, and the procurement of it will substantiate this.

Be not a slave to money or its uses.

Let money be your faithful servant sent forth to bring back dividends of joy, peace, happiness, and love.

Money seals a legitimate transaction.

Money serves as a medium of exchange and is nothing more than a highly evolved barter system.

Money is not security and cannot buy security.

Money will make no guarantees.

Money is putty in the hands of unscrupulous manipulators.

Money rejoices in the hands of wisdom.

Security is in the consciousness not in the possession of things or the accumulation of substance.

Do you believe it?

Can you accept it?

Is it easy?

No, it is not easy.

How well my soul remembers it was not easy.

Think!

Think for yourself.

Thoughts Let not the world with her cheap glitter, false glamour, and large scale promotions tempt you.

The world is a clever salesman living on commission.

The world is persuasive in all ways.

Be of good courage. You, too, can overcome the world.

Let not her trickery fool you or beat you with her treachery.

Man is a transmitter for the All-knowing Mind of the universe.

Keep all wave lengths clear so knowledge can be received without offensive static.

We are the sons of God, set for fine tuning.

Follow not man's reading of the stars but follow your own star of illumination that shines eternal within you.

Follow this eternal light.

Illumination is a true guide and will lead you to the manger of love.

In the stable of quietness, the Christ will find birth within your mind.

Bring your gifts.

Bring yourself.

This is the gift He seeks.

Jesus had His star, but He claimed Himself to be "The light of the world," not that which shone outside self.

You are the light of your world, and you will not walk in darkness if you let your light shine.

Let it be a guide on your path.

Yes, friend, let your light shine.

Let it shine on the path of another until his own light is bright enough to show the way.

Reincarnation is a spiritual annuity.

Reincarnation

Reincarnation deposits man into the bank of life as God's investment.

Man is given the tools of thought and feeling to shape and mold the dividends and in order to receive the highest good from this investment, God continues to reinvest Himself in man through the process known as reincarnation.

Soul makes her consent to withdraw her deposit and does so until such time she feels the need to circulate as usable substance.

Reincarnation allows man all the time he needs to make a personal encounter with God — that real self, the self of us that God became in order to build a kingdom in which His ideas of goodness would become a reality.

This book presents a soul journey.

You may discover a journey you, too, have taken.

Let it stimulate your thinking.

"Awake thou that sleepest," awake!

Your time has come for the realization of self.

Yes, I am traveling with you, beside you, and prayerfully supporting you on the flight in time and space.

Step by step, we are launching out into the deep, opening the sails of our minds to the winds of revelation.

Together, let us cast our nets into the sea of understanding and bring forth ideas of fulfillment.

All in all, it has been a pleasant journey with God as our agent.

The journey is exciting, and it is what you make it.

Plan your trip with a reliable company — the company of God.

Yes, as my soul has remembered, so must yours, and in this remembrance your questions will find answers.

I asked of life a little;
She paid a just amount.
I asked of life a lot,
And that is what I got.

Have no fear in asking,
Whatever it may be.
The wells of His abundance
Flow on full and free.

Ask of life the greatest,
Freely she will give.
Ask of life the answers,
Then truly will you live.

Journey

To sleep!
Then awake and find,
God has added
another link
in the
dimension of
the mind.
To rest!
Then wait, the opening
of another gate.
The soul
continues on
it's journey
with each dawn.

Joy -	God releasing Himself on the inner planes of Being in a union that brings man into true communion.
Peace -	The Silence of Self free from all outer distractions.
Love -	Life giving of itself on all planes and levels of consciousness.